HILLSIDE PUBLIC LIBRARY

3 1992 00163 8486

JUN 21 2007

W9-AEM-175

HILLSIDE PUBLIC LIBRARY
405 N. HILLSIDE AVENUE
HILLSIDE, IL 60162
(708) 449-7510

COLLEGE LIBRARY
HUMBER
COLLEGE BLVD.
10.

Beastly Bugs

Lynn Huggins-Cooper

A+
Smart Apple Media

Hillside Public Library

First published in 2005 by Franklin Watts
96 Leonard Street, London EC2A 4XD

Franklin Watts Australia
Hachette Children's Books
Level 17/207 Kent Street, Sydney NSW 2000

This edition published under license from Franklin Watts. All rights reserved.
Copyright © 2005 Franklin Watts

Editor: Jennifer Schofield
Art Director and Jacket Designer: Peter Scoulding
Designer: Jay Young
Picture researcher: Diana Morris

Acknowledgements:
Ingo Arndt/FLPA: front cover cl. Ingo Arndt/Nature PL: 6. Stephen
Ausmus/ARS/USDA: 14. Barb Backes: 29. Anthony Bannister/NHPA:
front cover bl, 10. Scott Bauer/ARS/USDA: 5, 13. Scott Bauer/USDA/
ARS/insectimages.org: 12. Mark Edwards/Still Pictures: 22b.
FogdenPhotos.com: 1, 25. Gautier/Still Pictures: 18. Wernher Krutein/
Photovault: 15. Dennis Kunkel/OSF: 21. E.K.Lorenz/SPL: 28. Ken Preston-
Mafham/Premaphotos: 11,16. Rod Preston-Mafham/Premaphotos: 24.
Jack Milchanowski/Ecoscene: front cover r, 26, 27. OSF: 4, 17, 19.
Peter Oxford/Nature PL: 7. Hans Pfletschinger/Still Pictures: 20.
Kjell Sandved/Ecoscene: 9. Jane Shemilt/SPL: 22cl. Sinclair Stammers/SPL: 23.

Published in the United States by Smart Apple Media
2140 Howard Drive West, North Mankato, Minnesota 56003

U.S. publication copyright © 2007 Smart Apple Media
International copyright reserved in all countries. No part of this book may
be reproduced in any form without written permission from the publisher.

Printed in the United States of America

Library of Congress Cataloging-in-Publication Data

Huggins-Cooper, Lynn.
Beastly bugs / by Lynn Huggins-Cooper.
p. cm. — (Killer nature)
ISBN-13 : 978-1-58340-936-7
1. Insects—Juvenile literature. 2. Insect pests—Juvenile literature. 3 Poisonous arthropoda—Juvenile literature.
I. Title.

QL467.2.H84 2006
595.7—dc22   2005056350

9 8 7 6 5 4 3 2 1

Contents

Beastly bugs   4

Spiky puss caterpillars   6

More about puss caterpillars   8

Stinging Africanized bees   10

More about killer bees   12

Ferocious fire ants   14

Deadly assassin bugs   16

High-jumping fleas   18

Buzzing mosquitoes   20

More about mosquitoes   22

Beastly blister beetles   24

Giant desert scorpions   26

Ancient bark scorpions   28

Key words   30

Web links   31

Index   32

Beastly bugs

Insects and other creepy crawlies are all around us. Scientists believe that there are nearly 8.5 million species of bugs in the world, including insects and arachnids. This book looks at some of the more beastly bugs around.

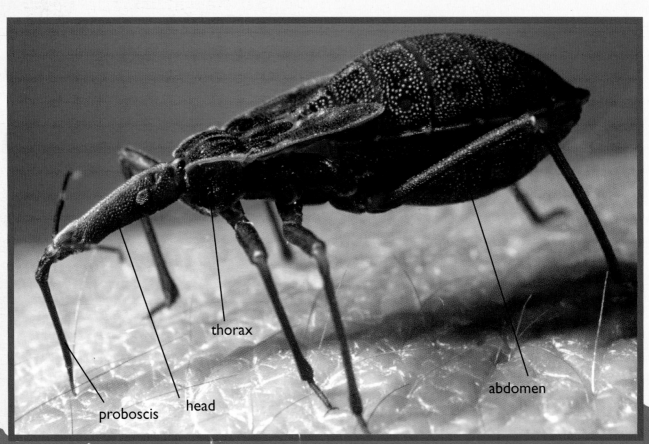

proboscis   head   thorax   abdomen

Bug facts

All insects have six legs. Their bodies are made up of three parts—the head, thorax, and abdomen. Most insects start life as an egg. Once they hatch, they go through a few changes before they become adults.

Arachnids have eight legs and two parts to their bodies. Arachnids do not go through the same changes insects do before they become adults. Instead, arachnids—such as the scorpions in this book—molt, or shed their skin.

Friend or foe?

There are all kinds of harmless bugs in the world, such as fireflies and ladybugs. But not all bugs are friendly.

Dangerous killer bugs such as Africanized bees (left), bark scorpions, and mosquitoes can sting, bite, and cause deadly diseases such as malaria.

Can you tell the difference between a harmless bug and a killer creepy crawly? Read on to find out more about these small beasts—it just might save your life one day!

Spiky puss caterpillars

The puss caterpillar is the larva of the flannel moth. These fluffy-looking creepy crawlies are found in the United States—including Texas, Maryland, Florida, and Missouri—and in Mexico. They are herbivores, and they feed on the leaves of elm, oak, plum, rose, wild cherry, holly, and sycamore trees.

Fact!

In Mexico, these furry bugs are called *el perrito*, which means "little dog."

Vital statistics

Puss caterpillars are quite small. They grow up to only one and a half inches (3.6 cm) long. They are covered in long, silky hairs. Under the hairs are short, hollow spikes. If you touch the hairs, the spikes break off into your skin, injecting venom.

When caterpillars sting

Out of 50 types of stinging caterpillars found in the U.S., puss caterpillars are the most poisonous. However, they use their poisonous spikes to protect themselves rather than to attack other animals. Puss caterpillars can sting even when they are dead. This encourages other animals to avoid them.

More about puss caterpillars

Encounters with people

People who touch puss caterpillars are in for a painful surprise. Once the spikes have injected their poison, there is a burning feeling, and the sting starts to swell. The victim may also have cramps, a headache, and a fever, and feel like vomiting. If you are stung by one of these nasty bugs, you should wash the irritated area as soon as possible. This will take away any spikes and poison left in the skin. Holding ice on the area will help with the pain and swelling.

Fact!

The painfulness of a sting depends on the caterpillar's size—bigger caterpillars have more painful stings.

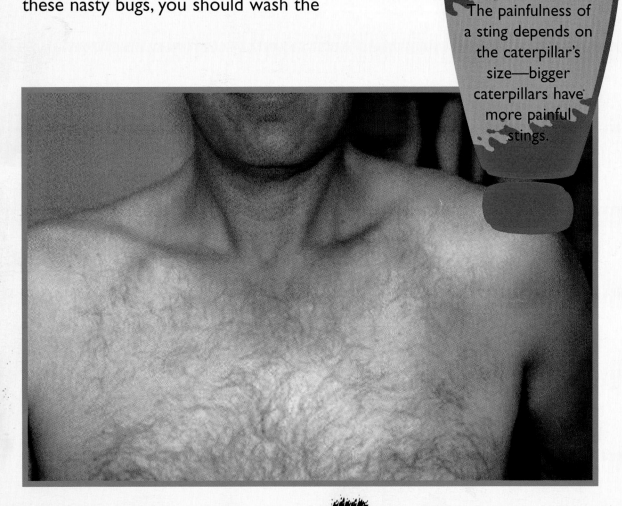

Survival

Puss caterpillars are not endangered. In Texas, in 1923 and 1954, there were very large numbers of caterpillars, and many people were stung.

There may have been so many caterpillars because there were low numbers of predators, such as birds, during those years.

Life cycle of a caterpillar

In the late spring or early summer, flannel moths lay eggs on leaves. After a few days, larvae hatch from the eggs. Within weeks, the larvae grow into hairy puss caterpillars. The caterpillars do not build cocoons (silky coverings). Instead, they change into moths inside their own skin. When this happens, the caterpillars look dead—but they are in fact pupating (changing from a caterpillar pupa into a moth). The caterpillars stay like this through the winter. In the spring, they break out of their old skin as adult moths.

Stinging Africanized bees

In 1956, fierce African bees were taken to Brazil to breed with European honey bees. Beekeepers hoped the new Africanized bees would make more honey than European bees in Brazil's hot weather.

The Africanized bees were accidentally released into the wild. They have spread quickly. In 1990, they were found in the U.S. in Texas, and by 1999, they had spread as far as California.

Vital statistics

Africanized honey bees look similar to European bees, but they are a little smaller. They are about three-quarters of an inch (2 cm) long. Only the female worker bees have a poisonous stinger on their abdomen. These bees live together in groups called colonies. They also swarm out together to find pollen and nectar.

Encounters with people

Africanized honey bees are not more poisonous than European bees; they are just more likely to attack. The bees are also easily disturbed—the sound of a lawn mower nearby is enough to make them attack.

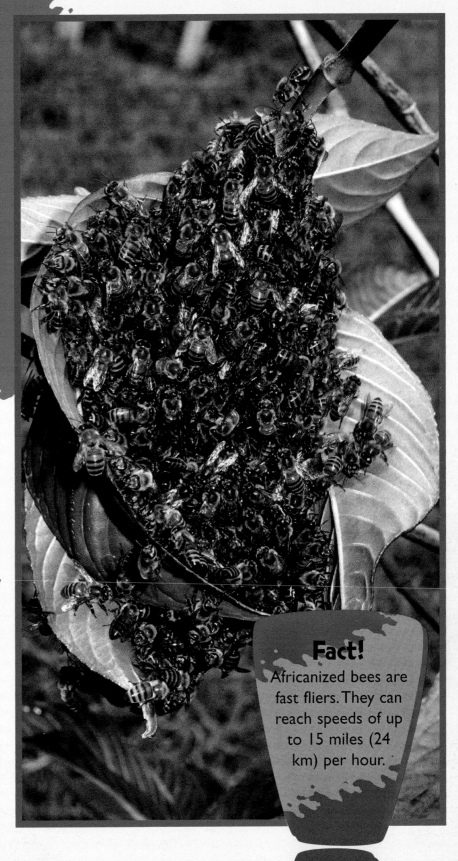

Fact!

Africanized bees are fast fliers. They can reach speeds of up to 15 miles (24 km) per hour.

More about killer bees

When bees attack

Africanized honey bees are known for attacking people. They are also called killer bees. Often, hundreds of killer bees can swarm out to sting at the same time. Beekeepers wear gloves and masks because the bees sting several times once they have a victim.

Killer bees can chase their victims for up to half a mile (800 m) before stinging them. The stings are quite painful, and they can be fatal for people who are allergic to bee stings. They can also be deadly for young or old people who cannot escape fast enough.

Real-life stories

In 1991, Jesus Diaz of Texas was attacked while mowing his lawn. He escaped with 18 stings. Another victim was not so lucky. In 1993, 82-year-old Lino Lopez died on his ranch. He was stung 40 times as he removed a colony of bees from a wall.

Survival

Africanized bees are not endangered— in fact, they are spreading fast. Each year, they spread another 200 miles (320 km). Africanized bees can travel up to 50 miles (80 km) to form new colonies and to find food. European bees usually move only a couple of miles.

Life cycle of a bee

Africanized honey bees grow from egg to adult quicker than European honey bees. Each colony has one queen bee. It is her job to lay eggs in cells made of beeswax. She can lay an amazing 1,500 eggs each day. About three days after being laid, the eggs develop into larvae. The larvae look like rice. They have no legs, wings, antennae, or eyes. They feed for a few days before becoming pupae. It takes just three weeks for the pupae to become adult bees.

Hillside Public Library

Ferocious fire ants

Fire ants were originally from South America. Now, they are found across the world in warm and tropical places, such as parts of the U.S., Africa, and Asia. There are several different species of fire ants, and it is hard to tell the difference between them and house or garden ants.

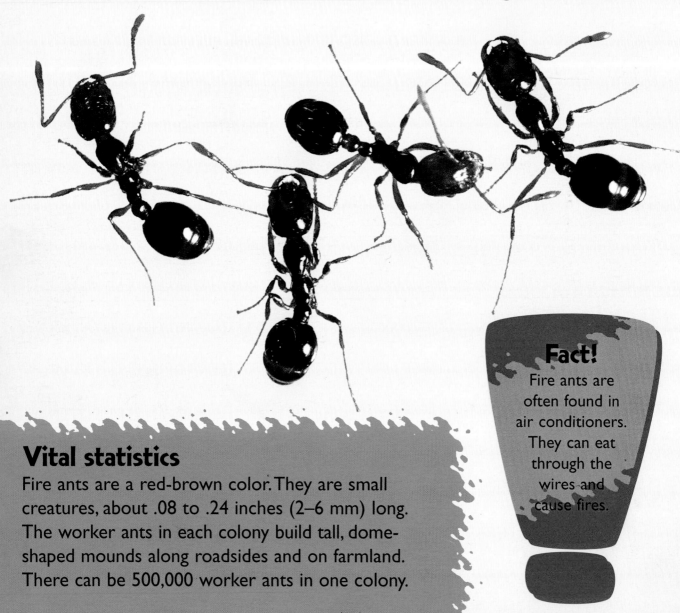

Vital statistics
Fire ants are a red-brown color. They are small creatures, about .08 to .24 inches (2–6 mm) long. The worker ants in each colony build tall, dome-shaped mounds along roadsides and on farmland. There can be 500,000 worker ants in one colony.

Fact!
Fire ants are often found in air conditioners. They can eat through the wires and cause fires.

Survival

Fire ants are very common and often infest an area. They are hard to get rid of; the pesticides used to kill them do not always work.

Life cycle of a fire ant

The queen ant lays eggs. She can lay up to 800 eggs a day. The eggs hatch in 6 to 10 days. After this, the larvae pupate. Adult fire ants emerge up to 15 days later.

How they kill

Fire ants eat carrion. They will also kill insects and small animals. These nasty bugs have even been known to attack foals and calves that are too young to run away. The ants kill by hanging on with their sharp jaws as they use their stingers to inject venom into their prey.

When fire ants sting

Fire ants get their name because their stings burn. The sting causes an itchy blister that can easily become infected. What makes fire ants especially dangerous is that many of them can attack at the same time. Since the 1930s, these vicious ants have killed about 60 people in the U.S.

Deadly assassin bugs

There are many different species of assassin bugs. They are found from South America to North America, Africa, and Australia. They are also known as kissing bugs because they pierce the lips, eyelids, and ears of their prey.

Vital statistics

Assassin bugs have flat bodies and small, cone-shaped heads. Adults are normally about three-quarters of an inch (2 cm) long, but they may grow up to two inches (5 cm). These stinging insects have a long, sharp proboscis that they use to stab their victims' skin.

Life cycle of an assassin bug

Female assassin bugs usually lay their eggs near leaves or in cracks. The eggs hatch in 10 to 30 days. The baby assassin bugs, or nymphs, shed their skin five times as they grow into adults. This takes about a year.

16

How they kill

Assassin bugs get their name because they pounce suddenly on their prey. They feed on the blood of mammals, such as humans and rats, as well as insects. They also carry parasites that can pass on diseases to humans. One such disease is Chagas disease.

Chagas disease is spread when a bug's waste infects a wound. Victims get a fever and swollen lymph nodes. The sickness can also damage people's heart and intestines. From Mexico to southern Argentina, 50,000 people die each year from Chagas disease.

When assassin bugs bite

These killer bugs hide in cracks in walls and ceilings during the day. At night, they creep out from their hiding places to suck the blood of sleeping humans. They feed for about 8 to 15 minutes.

Many people say that they did not feel the assassin bug's bite, but the bitten area can become very itchy and swollen. Victims often feel faint or sick. They may also have diarrhea and an allergic reaction to the bite.

High-jumping fleas

Fleas are wingless, blood-sucking pests. They are found throughout the world, mainly on pets such as cats and dogs. These vampire-like insects are as happy to bite humans as they are to bite pets.

Vital statistics

Fleas are tiny. They measure .08 to .3 inches (2–8 mm) long. They are oval-shaped and red-brown in color. Fleas have very strong back legs, which they use to jump onto victims. They can jump up to 7 inches (18 cm) high and 13 inches (33 cm) across. If a person jumped in the same way, he or she would jump 250 feet (76 m) high and 450 feet (137 m) across—that is as high as a 25-story building!

Life cycle of a flea

Female fleas lay between 15 and 20 eggs each day—that is about 600 in a lifetime. The eggs take between 2 and 14 days to hatch. When they hatch, the larvae look like tiny worms. They spin silken cocoons that are a quarter of an inch (.5 cm) long. The larvae pupate inside the cocoons and come out as adult fleas.

How they feed

These blood-sucking bugs have small antennae that feel heat and carbon dioxide. Carbon dioxide is given off when people and animals breathe. The antennae help fleas find a victim, such as a dog, a cat, or a person. The fleas jump onto the victim and bite at its flesh. As they do this, they inject a substance to make the blood they are drinking flow more easily. The bites make small, itchy bumps. The bites can also become infected.

Encounters with people

These tiny bugs can quickly infest a house. In a month, 10 female fleas can lay enough eggs to produce more than 250,000 young fleas. If you go on vacation and leave eggs to hatch, hundreds of fleas will be waiting for your warm body when you get home!

Flea bites give people diseases such as the bubonic plague. During the Middle Ages, this plague, known as the Black Death, killed more than 200 million people. Today, it can be cured by medicine.

Buzzing mosquitoes

Although they are tiny, mosquitoes are one of the most dangerous types of insects in the world. Each year, they kill between two and three million people by giving them deadly diseases such as malaria.

Vital statistics
Mosquitoes are small but deadly. They are about half an inch (1.25 cm) long and weigh about .00007 ounces (2 mg).

When mosquitoes bite

Male mosquitoes live on nectar from flowers and are harmless. However, the females live on blood, and their bites can be deadly. Blood gives the females the protein they need to be able to lay eggs. Like fleas, these blood-thirsty beasts find their victims by feeling the carbon dioxide gas that animals—as well as humans—give off as they breathe. Once they find a victim, they use their strong proboscis to bite into the flesh and suck blood.

Fact!
Mosquitoes' wings beat 500 times a second. You can hear the buzzing noise the wings make.

More about mosquitoes

Encounters with people

Mosquitoes breed in still water found in water storage tanks and drains. These are often near to where people live. In tropical regions, mosquitoes can give humans a wide range of harmful diseases, such as malaria, yellow fever, dengue, and encephalitis. In cooler regions, mosquitoes are a nuisance but usually are not deadly. Their bites leave itchy bumps that take time to heal.

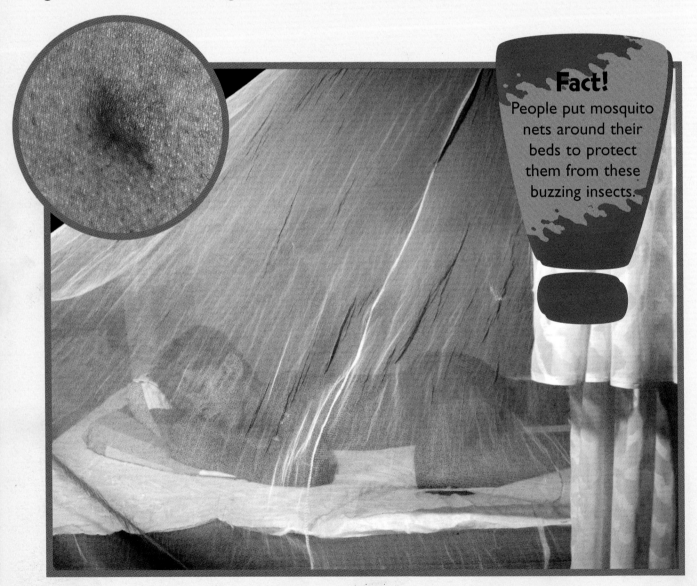

Fact!
People put mosquito nets around their beds to protect them from these buzzing insects.

Survival

People take great pains to kill these creatures because they carry such dangerous diseases. Insect repellent can help keep mosquitoes from biting. People can also take anti-malaria tablets to prevent malaria.

Some people also use harmful chemicals, called insecticides, to kill mosquitoes. The insecticides work well at first, and the mosquitoes are killed. But, after a while, the mosquitoes become used to them, and they stop working.

Life cycle of a mosquito

Female mosquitoes lay batches of between 100 and 300 eggs in water. They can lay from 1,000 to 3,000 eggs in a lifetime. The eggs turn into larvae, which look a bit like commas.

The larvae live under the water's surface. They breathe through an air tube like a snorkel. Once they are adults, they leave the water. In warm weather, mosquitoes can reach adulthood in just seven days.

Beastly blister beetles

Blister beetles are found all over the world. They get their name because they give off a poisonous oil that causes blisters if it comes into contact with human skin.

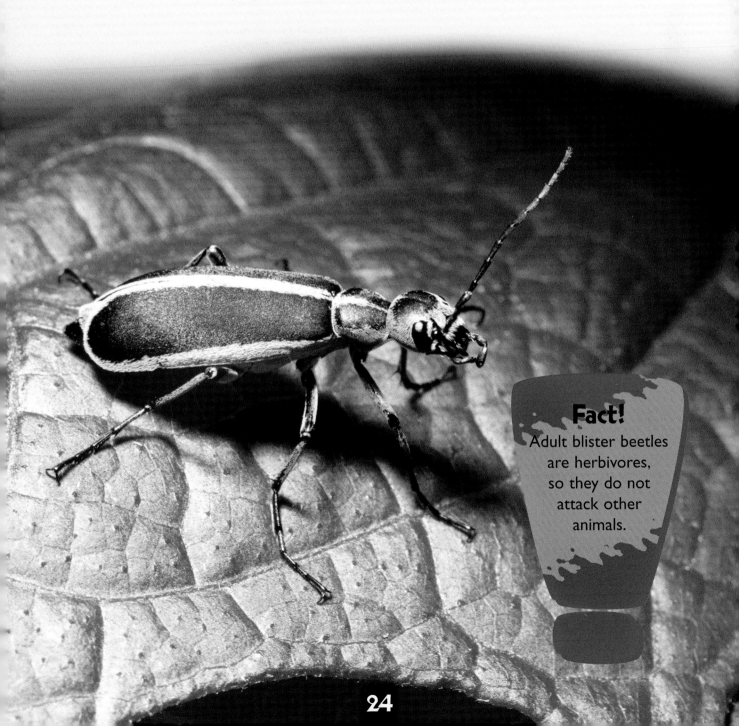

Fact!
Adult blister beetles are herbivores, so they do not attack other animals.

Life cycle of a blister beetle

In the summer, female blister beetles lay eggs in soil. Tiny larvae hatch out of the eggs. They wander around looking for grasshopper eggs on which to feed. As they become older, the larvae lose their legs and look more like maggots.

By the winter, the larvae develop a thick, protective skin. They bury themselves in soil, and they stay there until the spring. In the spring-time, they come out from under the soil as adult blister beetles.

Vital statistics

Blister beetles are between three-quarters of an inch and one and a quarter inches (2–3 cm) long. They have broad heads and long antennae, which they use to find their way around.

Beetle juice

Blister beetles give off a very poisonous liquid, called cantharidin oil. When this oil touches the skin of animals, including humans, it causes irritating blisters. In humans, cantharidin oil can cause the kidneys to stop working, and it can also cause death.

Sometimes blister beetles give off their deadly oil in hay. Animals such as cows, sheep, and horses then eat the hay without realizing that it has cantharidin oil in it. The cantharidin oil irritates the animals' stomachs, and it can even kill the animals.

Giant desert scorpions

Giant desert scorpions are the largest scorpions found in the U.S. They live in the deserts of California, Arizona, southern Utah, and Nevada, as well as in Mexico.

These large creatures are also known as giant hairy scorpions because of the brown hairs on their bodies.

Fact!

Scorpions may be beastly, but they are not insects. They are arachnids, like spiders.

Vital statistics

Like all arachnids, giant desert scorpions have eight legs. They also have powerful, pincer-like claws and a tail that ends in a sharp, hollow stinger. Giant desert scorpions grow up to six inches (15 cm) long.

How they kill

Giant desert scorpions are carnivorous. They eat insects, spiders, centipedes, lizards, and other smaller scorpions. During the day, the scorpions hide under rocks or in burrows. At night, they wait for prey. They use their body hairs to feel for vibrations in the air and ground. This tells them when prey and predators are nearby. They lie waiting for prey, and as soon as it is spotted, they pounce on it with their pincers. Using their long stinger, they paralyze their victim. They then tear the prey apart with their pincers.

Encounters with people

Although this scorpion is often kept as a pet, it can give a painful sting. Unless you are allergic to the scorpion's venom, the sting will not kill you, but it will cause pain and swelling. During the summer, these beastly bugs may be found hiding in sleeping bags and other dark places around homes and garages.

Baby desert scorpions

Female giant desert scorpions give birth to between 25 and 35 live young. The mother makes a birth basket with her legs, catching the young as they are born. The newborn babies climb up the female's pincers onto her back. The mother then carries them for a couple of weeks until they molt for the first time. After this, they are able to look after themselves.

Ancient bark scorpions

Bark scorpions are one of the most dangerous types of scorpions in the U.S. They are found in southern and western Arizona, southern Utah, and southern Nevada, as well as in Mexico. Bark scorpions live in dark places. They hide during the day and become active at night.

Fact!
Fossils from millions of years ago show that scorpions have not changed much since they first appeared on Earth.

Vital statistics
Bark scorpions are small compared with giant desert scorpions. On average, adults measure two to two and three-quarter inches (5–7 cm) long, including their curved tail.

How they kill

Bark scorpions are carnivorous. They eat mainly small insects, which they tear apart with their pincers. Larger prey is stung first, and venom is injected into the victim's body. The scorpions partly digest their prey with juices from their mouth before they suck the mushy food into their stomach.

Baby bark scorpions

Before the male and female bark scorpion mate, they perform a "dance." The male holds the female's pincers and twirls her around for hours before mating. After that, about 30 eggs develop inside the mother's body.

Several months later, baby bark scorpions hatch out of the eggs. The young ride on their mother's back for about a week until they molt for the first time.

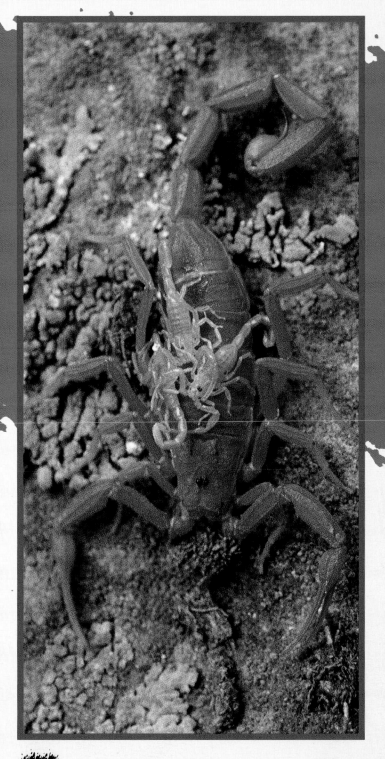

Pamela the goat

Bark scorpions have a deadly sting. Each year in Mexico, a few people die from their stings. However, in Arizona, there have been no bark scorpion-related deaths for more than 30 years. This is because of a goat named Pamela. Pamela is injected with tiny doses of venom, and her blood is used to produce bark scorpion antivenin.

Key words

Abdomen
The lower part of an insect's body.

Aggressive
Dangerous and likely to attack for no reason.

Antivenin
The medicine given to fight the effect of venom—it is sometimes called an antidote.

Arachnids
Animals that have eight legs, no wings or antennae, and a body divided into two parts. Scorpions, spiders, and mites are arachnids.

Bubonic plague
A deadly sickness carried by fleas. People with bubonic plague have a fever and diarrhea, and they vomit.

Carbon dioxide
A gas in the air given off when animals and people breathe.

Carnivorous
Animals that eat meat are carnivorous.

Carrion
The rotting flesh of dead animals.

Colony
A group of insects.

Endangered
When a group of animals is in danger of dying out completely, it is endangered.

Fatal
When something ends in death.

Herbivores
Animals that eat only plants.

Insect repellent
Creams, sprays, and oils used to keep insects from biting.

Larva
An insect in the early stage of its growth. The plural of larva is larvae.

Life cycle
An insect's change in growth from an egg, into a larva, into a pupa, and into an adult. The adult lays eggs, and the cycle starts again.

Lymph nodes
Parts inside our bodies that help to filter infectious substances from the blood.

Parasites
Animals, such as fleas, that live off other animals.

Pesticide
A chemical used to kill insects.

Predator
An animal that hunts and eats other animals.

Prey
Animals hunted by other animals for food.

Proboscis
A needle-like body part found on some insects; it is used for sucking and feeding.

Pupa
The stage in an insect's growth after it is a larva.

Pupating
When an insect changes from a larva into an adult, it is pupating.

Species
A group of living things that can breed with one another.

Thorax
The middle part of an insect's body.

Venom
Poison or toxins.

Web links

http://www.giantscreenbugs.com/
Have lots of fun with these 3-D bug animations.

http://www.daniellesplace.com/html/bugs.html
Great bug things to make.

http://exoticpets.about.com/cs/insectsspiders/a/invertebratepet.htm
All the information and tips you need to keep bugs as pets.

http://www.ecokids.ca/pub/fun_n_games/games/bugHunt/index.cfm
Hunt the bugs with this fun game.

http://www.butterfliesnbugs.com
Join a club with people who are interested in bugs.

http://www.enchantedlearning.com/themes/insects.shtml
Features lots of information and activity sheets on bugs.

Note to parents:
Every effort has been made to ensure that the Web sites in this book are suitable for children, that they are of the highest educational value, and that they contain no inappropriate or offensive material. However, due to the nature of the Internet, it is impossible to guarantee that the contents of these sites will not be altered. We strongly advise that Internet access be supervised by a responsible adult.

Index

abdomens 4, 11, 30
Africa 14, 16
antennae 13, 19, 25, 30
antivenin 29, 30
arachnids 4, 26, 30
Argentina 17
Asia 14
assassin bugs (kissing bugs)
    16–17
Australia 16

bee keepers 10, 12
bees
  African honey 10
  Africanized honey
    (killer bees) 5, 10–13
  European honey 10, 11, 13
birth baskets 27
bites and biting 17, 19, 21, 22,
    23, 30
blister beetles 24–25
blisters 15, 24, 25
blood 17, 18, 19, 21, 29, 30, 31
Brazil 10
bubonic plague 19, 30

cantharidin oil 25
carbon dioxide 19, 21, 30
carrion 15, 30
Chagas disease 17
cocoons 9, 19
colonies 11, 13, 14, 30

dengue 22
desert 26
Diaz, Jesus 13

eggs 4, 9, 13, 15, 16, 19, 21, 23,
    25, 29, 30
endangered species 9, 13, 30
eyes 13, 16

fever 8, 17, 30
fire ants 14–15
fireflies 5
flannel moths 6, 9
fleas 18–19, 30, 31
flowers 11, 13, 21
fossils 28

hairs 7, 9, 26, 27
hay 25
heads 4, 16, 25
herbivores 6, 24, 30
honey 10

insect repellents 23, 30
insecticides 23

ladybugs 5
larvae 6, 9, 13, 19, 23, 25, 30, 31
leaves 6, 9, 16
legs 4, 13, 18, 25, 26, 27, 30
life cycles 4, 9, 13, 15, 16, 19,
    23, 25, 30
lips 16
Lopez, Lino 13
lymph nodes 17, 30

malaria 5, 22, 23
  anti-malaria tablets 23
mammals 17, 21
mating 29
Mexico 6, 17, 26, 28, 29
Middle Ages 19
molting 4, 27, 29
mosquito nets 22
mosquitoes 5, 20–23
mouths 29

nectar 11, 21
North America 16
nymphs 16

Pamela the goat 29
parasites 17, 31
people 8, 11, 12, 15, 17, 18, 19,
    20, 21, 22, 23, 24, 25, 27
pesticides 15, 31
pets 18, 27
pincers 26, 27, 29
poison and venom 7, 8, 9, 11,
    15, 24, 25, 27, 29, 30, 31
pollen 11, 13
predators 9, 27, 31
prey 15, 16, 17, 27, 29, 31
proboscis 16, 21, 31
pupas and pupating 9, 13, 15,
    19, 30, 31
puss caterpillars 6–9

queens 13

scorpions 4, 30
  bark 5, 28–29
  giant desert (hairy) scorpions
    26–27, 28
skin 7, 9, 16, 24, 25
South America 14, 16
spikes 7, 8
stingers and stings 7, 8, 11, 12,
    13, 15, 16, 26, 27, 29
stomachs 25, 29
swarms 12

tails 26, 28
thorax 4, 31

U.S. 6, 7, 9, 10, 13, 14, 15, 26,
    28, 29

waste 17
water 22, 23
wings 13, 21, 30
worker ants 14